ANIMAL HEROES OF WORLD WAR II

First published in Great Britain and the United States
in 2026 by Welbeck Children's Books
An imprint of Hachette Children's Group

Author: Jules Attwell

A CIP catalogue record for this book is available from the British Library.

ISBN 978 1 83955 416 2
Printed in China
10 9 8 7 6 5 4 3 2 1

Welbeck Children's Books
An imprint of Hachette Children's Group
Part of Hodder & Stoughton Limited
Carmelite House, 50 Victoria Embankment
London EC4Y 0DZ

The authorised representative in the EEA is Hachette Ireland, 8 Castlecourt Centre, Castleknock Road, Castleknock, Dublin 15, D15 YF6A, Ireland (email: info@hbgi.ie).

A Hachette UK Company
www.hachette.co.uk
www.hachettechildrens.co.uk

ANIMAL HEROES OF WORLD WAR II

CONTENTS

ANIMAL HEROES OF WWII

We often picture World War II as tanks rumbling across battlefields, planes roaring through the sky, and soldiers marching into danger.

But the story of the war is not just about people and machines.

Countless animals worked alongside their human partners. Dogs guarded camps and sniffed out danger. Pigeons carried secret messages across enemy lines, and horses and mules hauled heavy supplies across rough terrain. Even cats boosted morale, offering comfort to weary troops far from home.

These animals' contributions are often overlooked, but they were heroes, too. This is their story.

PDSA
For Gallantry

DOGS ON THE FRONT LINE

War is loud and chaotic, and in World War II many dogs were in the middle of it.

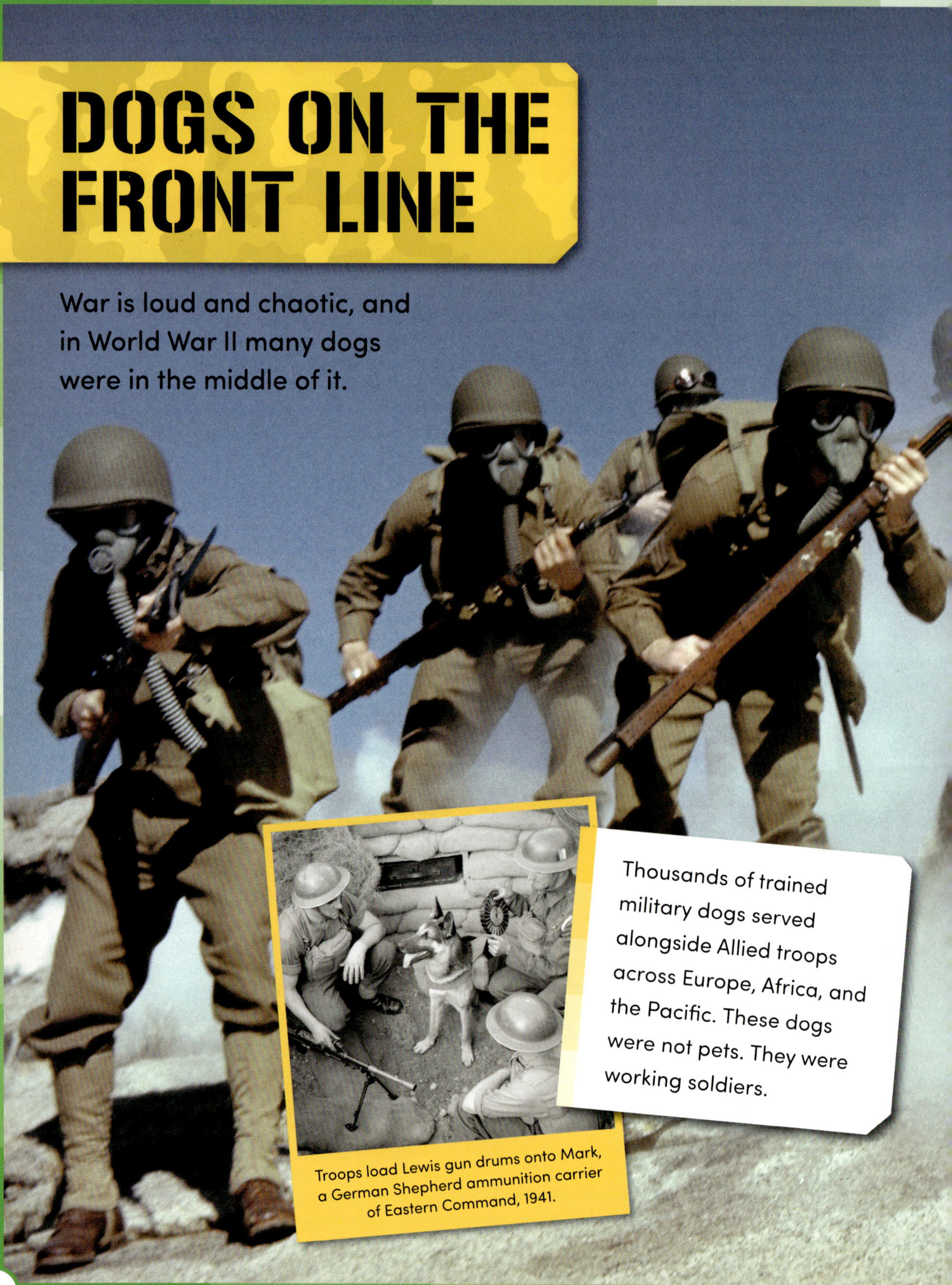

Troops load Lewis gun drums onto Mark, a German Shepherd ammunition carrier of Eastern Command, 1941.

Thousands of trained military dogs served alongside Allied troops across Europe, Africa, and the Pacific. These dogs were not pets. They were working soldiers.

January 1944, London, UK: Rescue dogs search the Royal Hospital Chelsea after a German V-2 strike.

Some dogs sniffed out hidden mines before soldiers stepped on them. Others searched bombed buildings for survivors trapped beneath debris. Messenger dogs ran through gunfire carrying notes between units when radios failed. Guard dogs stood watch at night, warning troops of approaching enemies.

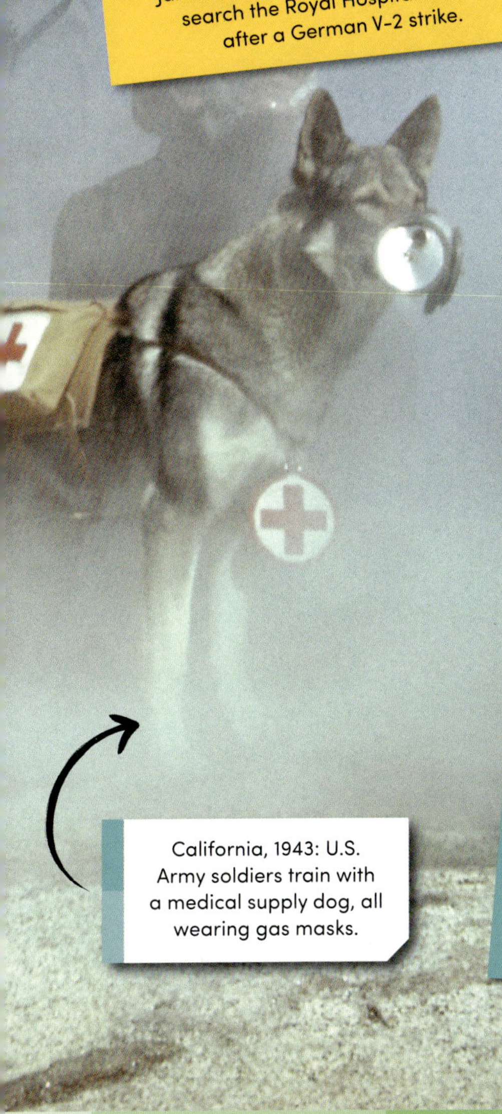

California, 1943: U.S. Army soldiers train with a medical supply dog, all wearing gas masks.

All dogs must be well trained to survive the noise and dangers of war.

TRAINING WAR DOGS

As the war escalated, the United States military realized dogs could play an important role.

September 1942: A German Shepherd leaps through two 12-inch (30 cm) hoops during training.

In 1942, a group called "Dogs for Defense" asked American families to donate their pet dogs for military service. Thousands of families responded. Soon after, the U.S. Army launched the "War Dog Program" with the "K-9 Corps."

German Shepherds, like this one, were trained by the U.S. Army during World War II.

These dogs were trained to obey commands, even amid noise and chaos. They learned to crawl, stay silent, and ignore distractions. Some were trained to detect mines or hidden enemies. Others became messengers, scouts, or guard dogs.

September 1942: A German Shepherd slides down an obstacle during pursuit training.

The bond between soldiers and working dogs is often strong.

IT'S A FACT!

The U.S. Marine Corps opened its own dog training center, where Doberman Pinschers became known as "Devil Dogs" in the Pacific.

Every dog was paired with a handler: a soldier who trained, fed, and lived with them. From family pets to battlefield partners, these dogs became soldiers in their own right.

A handler with his dog, similar to those used by the military in World War II.

SEARCH AND RESCUE DOGS

During the war, the PDSA organised some of the first rescue dog squads to search bomb-damaged buildings for people buried under rubble.

Beauty, a wire-haired fox terrier, is considered one of the earliest dogs to work with a PDSA rescue squad. Her success at finding people helped inspire the development of formal training methods.

A wire-haired Fox Terrier named Beauty serving with early PDSA rescue squads.

A Fox Terrier, a breed used in World War II search and rescue.

A PDSA terrier Beauty searches bomb-damaged rubble for trapped animals.

IT'S A FACT!

PDSA stands for People's Dispensary for Sick Animals. It was founded in the UK in 1917 to care for animals in need and, during the war, broadened its work to support rescue dogs.

Handlers learned to train dogs to ignore smoke, noise, and crowds, and to signal clearly when they found someone buried under debris.

A modern-day rescue dog.

These methods influenced modern search-and-rescue organisations. Today, both professional and volunteer rescue dog organisations still use structured scent training, handler bonding, and disaster simulation exercises that were first developed during World War II.

BRAVERY IN BURNING BUILDINGS

War doesn't only take place on the battlefield. It is often much closer to home.

During World War II, enemy bombing raids caused fires that left people trapped inside burning buildings. Rescue dogs were trained to search through the wreckage, helping to find those trapped.

London firefighters tackling fires after a night raid, c. 1941.

Rex, a Civil Defence rescue dog and recipient of the PDSA Dickin Medal.

Rex, a search and rescue dog, worked alongside his handlers when bombs set many parts of London on fire. Rex used his nose and sharp hearing to search through smoke, rubble, and twisted metal to find people trapped beneath the debris.

A modern search dog working through ruins after an earthquake.

IT'S A FACT

A trained search dog can detect human scent buried under layers of rubble.

December 1940, Holbrooks, Coventry, UK: Firefighters at work after a Luftwaffe raid.

DID YOU KNOW?

Dogs can hear sounds up to four times further away than humans can.

German Shepherds' sharp ears and keen noses make them ideal rescue dogs.

PARATROOPER DOGS

Alongside their human handlers, trained paratrooper dogs jumped from planes and landed behind enemy lines.

The Normandy coastline today, where Allied paratroopers landed on D-Day 1944.

Brian, a German Shepherd, became one of Britain's most famous paradogs during World War II. He served with the 13th Parachute Battalion, which landed in Normandy during the Allied invasion of France.

Paratrooper dogs jumped alongside soldiers, landing behind enemy lines during dangerous missions.

A PDSA Dickin Medal is awarded to war dog Brian by Sir Frederick Bowhill, London, UK, 1947.

Salvo, an airborne dog with the Parachute Regiment, wearing an American-designed harness.

A Finnish parachutist and dog jumping from aircraft, 1937.

Brian and other brave canines were trained to stay calm during flights and to get to work as soon as they landed. Paratrooper dogs could detect movement and danger long before soldiers did and helped guard camps and warn troops of approaching threats.

IT'S A FACT!

Dogs can hear sounds up to 45,000 vibrations per second, over twice as high as humans can hear.

THE P.O.W. DOG

Judy was an English Pointer and the ship's mascot on HMS Grasshopper in Asia.

When the British ship HMS Grasshopper was attacked near Singapore in 1942, Judy and the sailors managed to escape to a nearby island. The crew were desperate for fresh water. Judy discovered a fresh-water spring, helping the crew survive.

Later in the war, Judy was captured and smuggled into a Japanese prison camp in Medan, Indonesia. In the camp, Judy's life was in danger, but airman Frank Williams fought to protect her. He persuaded a camp commander to list Judy as an official prisoner of war.

Judy, the ship's mascot of HMS Grasshopper, survived the ship's sinking and was later held in a prisoner of war camp.

August 1946: Frank Williams grooms Judy before her PDSA Dickin Medal ceremony.

Judy is the only dog known to be formally registered as a World War II prisoner of war. Her P.O.W. I.D. was: 81A Gloegoer Medan.

Thousands of Allied soldiers were imprisoned in Japanese prisoner of war (P.O.W.) camps.

IT'S A FACT!

English Pointers were bred to "point" by freezing in place and pointing their nose toward hidden birds.

SNIFFING OUT DANGER

Dogs in World War II helped sniff out hidden danger. Their noses could detect explosives buried underground before soldiers reached them.

A landmine, one of the many hidden dangers of the battlefield.

One dog who helped keep soldiers safe was Ricky, a Welsh Collie.

Ricky entered the War Dogs Training School in Hertfordshire in 1944 and quickly proved he had the intelligence and temperament required for one of the toughest jobs a dog could do: detecting buried mines.

In December 1944, Ricky and his handler, Maurice Yielding, were assigned to clear mines along the Noordervaart Canal in the Netherlands.

DID YOU KNOW?

Many herding dogs use an intense stare called "the eye" to control sheep. Just one stare can make a whole flock move!

Time after time, Ricky located mines before soldiers stepped on them. But one explosion went off, and Ricky and Maurice were hit by shrapnel. Even though injured, they continued searching for mines nearby. Ricky's courage and loyalty made him a true animal hero of the war.

Ricky, a Royal Army Veterinary Corps mine-clearing dog, helped rescue Sergeant Maurice Yielding.

Hidden landmines were designed to explode when someone stepped on or disturbed them.

IT'S A FACT!

Dogs communicate using a mixture of body language, such as posture, tail position, ear movement, and eye contact, often without making any noise at all.

CANINE COURAGE

Gander, a Newfoundland dog, was the beloved mascot of the Royal Rifles of Canada.

In December 1941, during the Battle of Lye Mun on Hong Kong Island, Gander was seen rushing towards enemy soldiers, distracting them and helping protect his regiment, alongside the Winnipeg Grenadiers and other troops.

A Newfoundland similar to Gander, the mascot of a Canadian regiment.

Gander, the Newfoundland mascot of the 1st Battalion, Royal Rifles of Canada, 1940.

The Canadian flag, the national flag of the country served by the Royal Rifles of Canada.

The PDSA Dickin Medal recognizes their bravery in war.

Gander's final act of bravery came when he helped protect a group of soldiers during an enemy attack. The brave dog died while saving their lives. For his courage, Gander was later awarded the PDSA Dickin Medal, often called the animal Victoria Cross.

IT'S A FACT!

For hundreds of years, Newfoundlands have helped rescue people from the water, towing them to safety.

A modern Newfoundland during water work training.

DID YOU KNOW?

Newfoundlands have webbed feet and water-resistant coats, making them excellent swimmers.

WINGS OF WAR

In World War II, urgent messages could mean the difference between victory and disaster.

A Signal Corps radio operation by U.S. shore fire control group, Normandy, France, June 1944.

Armies used many machines to send messages, such as radios that transmitted voice and coded messages over long distances. Field telephones were connected by wires stretched between trenches and command posts, and signal lamps flashed Morse code messages.

But equipment could break, radio signals could be jammed, and wires could be cut.

A World War II military phone used to send messages.

When technology failed, a small but reliable helper often saved the day. Homing pigeons simply followed their instinct and flew home, carrying a message safely strapped to their leg.

A carrier pigeon released during U.S. Airborne training exercises, 1944.

A wartime carrier pigeon showing a message holder and identification ring, c. 1941.

Across Europe, North Africa, and the Pacific, these pigeons helped deliver crucial messages across enemy lines and provided a lifeline to soldiers when their equipment failed.

DID YOU KNOW?

Scientists believe pigeons can sense Earth's magnetic field to help guide their flight.

IT'S A FACT!

Pigeons have powerful chest muscles that allow them to fly long distances without stopping.

THE PIGEON WHO BEAT THE BOMBERS

In October 1943, Allied troops were advancing through Italy. In the village of Calvi Vecchia, British forces had already captured the town sooner than expected. But Allied planes were already on their way to bomb it.

Allied bombers like these flew missions against enemy targets.

The bombing needed to be stopped, but the airstrike was already planned and there wasn't enough time to send a message by normal channels.

So the soldiers turned to G.I. Joe, a homing pigeon with the U.S. Army Signal Corps.

A Swedish soldier with a carrier pigeon during World War II.

G.I. Joe was released with a note tied to his leg. He flew about 20 miles in 20 minutes straight to Allied headquarters.

The message arrived just in time, and the attack was called off, saving at least 100 soldiers.

Messenger pigeons could fly long distances to deliver urgent wartime messages.

G.I. Joe receiving the Dickin Medal at the Tower of London, UK, November 1946.

For his speed and lifesaving flight, G.I. Joe became the first US pigeon to receive the PDSA Dickin Medal for bravery.

A homing pigeon like G.I. Joe, one of the most famous wartime messenger birds.

IT'S A FACT!

Following his service, G.I. Joe lived out the rest of his life in the U.S. He was cared for at the Detroit Zoo, where he became something of a celebrity.

D-DAY DELIVERIES

On D-Day, 6 June 1944, Allied paratroopers landed behind enemy lines in Normandy. Radios were unreliable in the chaos of the landings, so soldiers released homing pigeons with urgent updates.

Airborne troopers descending.

One of those birds was the Duke of Normandy. The Duke served with the Army Pigeon Service and was the first pigeon to arrive in Britain with a message from the 21st Army Group in Normandy.

The PDSA Dickin Medal awarded to the Duke of Normandy for wartime bravery.

A carrier pigeon being presented with the PDSA Dickin Medal for wartime bravery.

The Duke's successful flight confirmed that the troops had landed and were holding their positions.

A homing pigeon similar to those used as message carriers during World War II.

Another remarkable pigeon was Paddy of the British Royal Air Force (RAF). Paddy carried a critical message from Normandy back to Britain, completing the journey across the English Channel in just over four hours, making it the fastest recorded pigeon flight of D-Day.

The carrier pigeon Paddy returning from Normandy, France, 1944.

1940s: Pigeons used as Britain's backup communication system.

IT'S A FACT!

Some homing pigeons can fly 500 miles (805 km), or more, in one day, which is approximately the distance from New York City to Detroit!

DID YOU KNOW?

D-Day means the day a military mission starts. The most famous D-Day was 6 June 1944.

SAVED FROM THE SEA

When aircraft were shot down over the sea, aircrews often found themselves stranded in small life rafts. Radios frequently failed, or were damaged in the crash. In those desperate moments, one small bird could mean survival.

1942: Messenger pigeon Winkie aided rescue after a North Sea bomber crash.

Signalmen prepare a carrier pigeon dispatch in Ballymena, July 1941.

Specially trained homing pigeons were often carried aboard aircraft so they could fly for help. One of those lifesaving pigeons was called Dutch Coast.

DID YOU KNOW?

Many World War II aircraft carried homing pigeons in case radios failed.

In April 1942, a British aircraft was forced to ditch in the sea near the enemy-held coast of the Netherlands. The radio was broken, so the crew released the pigeon with an urgent SOS message tied to its leg. The brave bird flew about 288 miles (463 km) across the North Sea to Britain in just a few hours, delivering a message that led rescuers to the stranded airmen.

Soldiers send a message using a carrier pigeon, 1940.

IT'S A FACT!

In winter, the North Sea can be as cold as 37°F (3°C), resulting in "cold shock" in just minutes. Cold shock happens when icy water makes your body gasp, and your breathing becomes hard to control.

Pigeons can fly at speeds of up to 80 mph (130 km/h).

WINGED WAR WARRIORS

It wasn't just pigeons who helped the war effort–other birds did, too!

Falcons and hawks were trained to hunt messenger pigeons used by enemy troops. These birds of prey are incredible fliers, able to dive through the sky at breathtaking speeds. Soldiers used these hunters to stop secret messages carried by pigeons from reaching their targets. One such bird was Ursula, a peregrine falcon.

Ursula, a trained peregrine falcon, swoops on a pigeon, June 1945.

A bald eagle, the national bird of the United States.

IT'S A FACT!

The bald eagle became the official national bird of the United States in 1782 and was widely used in WWII propaganda posters.

Out at sea, another group of birds played a vital role. Sailors often watched seabirds closely, knowing that large flocks sometimes gathered where submarines disturbed the water below. Because of this pattern, sharp-eyed crews learned that birds circling above the waves could signal something unusual was happening beneath the surface.

By simply following their natural instincts, these birds helped humans spot danger during the war.

Seagulls in flight above surfers at Maroubra Beach, Sydney, Australia.

Falcons were sometimes trained to intercept enemy messenger pigeons during World War II.

Falcons like this one were trained to intercept enemy messenger pigeons.

DID YOU KNOW?

Some falcons can dive at more than 200 mph (320 km/h), making them the fastest animals on earth.

HEROES ON HOOVES

World War II is often remembered as a war of tanks, trucks, and roaring engines. However, when roads turned to mud, heavy snow buried mountain passes, or dense forests blocked the way, Allied troops turned to four legs: horses, mules and donkeys.

A U.S. Army communications unit on horseback, 1940.

Soldiers with a horse-drawn wagon collect spent shells at a beach ammunition testing range, England, c. 1942.

These strong animals hauled heavy supplies and fuel, pulled artillery, and carried food and ammunition to soldiers on the front lines.

IT'S A FACT!

Draft horses are specifically bred to pull heavy loads, like wagons and artillery.

Sometimes horses traveled for miles through enemy territory, working under fire to deliver essential supplies. Their work rarely made headlines, but without them, armies would have struggled to move forward.

German supply wagons on the Lapland Front, summer 1943.

Horses carry packs of up to 320 lbs (145 kg) and act as transport for Special Service infantry, 1940.

DID YOU KNOW?

Horses and mules can travel safely over rocky trails and steep mountain paths where vehicles can't go.

HOOVES THROUGH THE BLITZ

In World War II, many horses worked with police in cities and towns, helping to keep order on the streets.

On July 3, 1944, a German V-1 flying bomb exploded in South London, destroying four houses.

A German V-1 rocket from World War II.

Olga carrying out her duties as a police horse in London, UK.

Police horse Olga was on duty nearby with her rider, Police Constable J. E. Thwaites, when a huge plate-glass window shattered and crashed down in front of her. Startled, Olga bolted 100 yards (90 metres).

P.C. Thwaites quickly calmed Olga, and they returned to the scene. Amid the smoke and debris, Olga stayed steady, directing traffic and helping rescue teams.

Olga's bravery was not forgotten and she was later awarded the PDSA Dickin Medal.

Police horses Regal, Olga, and Upstart at the Dickin Medal Award Ceremony, London, UK, June 1947.

IT'S A FACT!

Horses respond to subtle cues from their riders, including shifts in weight or gentle rein pressure.

FEARLESS IN THE FIRE

During air attacks, bombs did not just hit important buildings. They also struck homes, streets, police stations, and stables.

Regal was a Metropolitan Police horse stationed at Muswell Hill in London, where he lived in the stables.

During one air raid, incendiary bombs struck the stables and chaos erupted as flames and smoke filled the air. Regal was trapped inside the burning building. Although he suffered minor injuries, he remained remarkably calm, allowing officers to move all the horses to safety. Regal's calm bravery helped save the other horses.

Auxiliary fire men battle fires after a German air raid in London, UK, 1940.

One of the Metropolitan Police horses honored for bravery during the London Blitz, London, 1947.

Police horses like Regal played an important wartime role. They patroled streets during blackouts, helped control crowds after air raids, and supported civil defense operations. Today, police horses still patrol city streets and help officers manage large crowds, continuing the work horses like Regal once carried out during the war.

A modern mounted police officer patrols city streets.

Horses often take turns standing watch while herd-mates lie down to sleep.

IT'S A FACT!

Horses can sleep both lying down and standing up. Special muscles in their legs help them stay balanced while they rest.

DID YOU KNOW?

A horse's teeth keep growing throughout most of its life.

WAR'S FOUR-LEGGED WORKFORCE

Like many other animals during World War II, millions of horses, mules, and donkeys served with armies around the world.

In Eastern Europe, the Soviet and Polish armies used cavalry units that rode horses into battle.

Polish cavalry at the start of World War II preparing for battle.

Pack horses cross terrain impassable to vehicles, 1940.

Horses also hauled wagons carrying food, ammunition, and equipment.

German and Japanese forces relied heavily on horses to move supplies across long distances where muddy roads and freezing winters stopped many vehicles.

German troops transporting a mortar across water, 1939.

The United States Army depended on thousands of mules to carry equipment through mountains and jungles where trucks could not go.

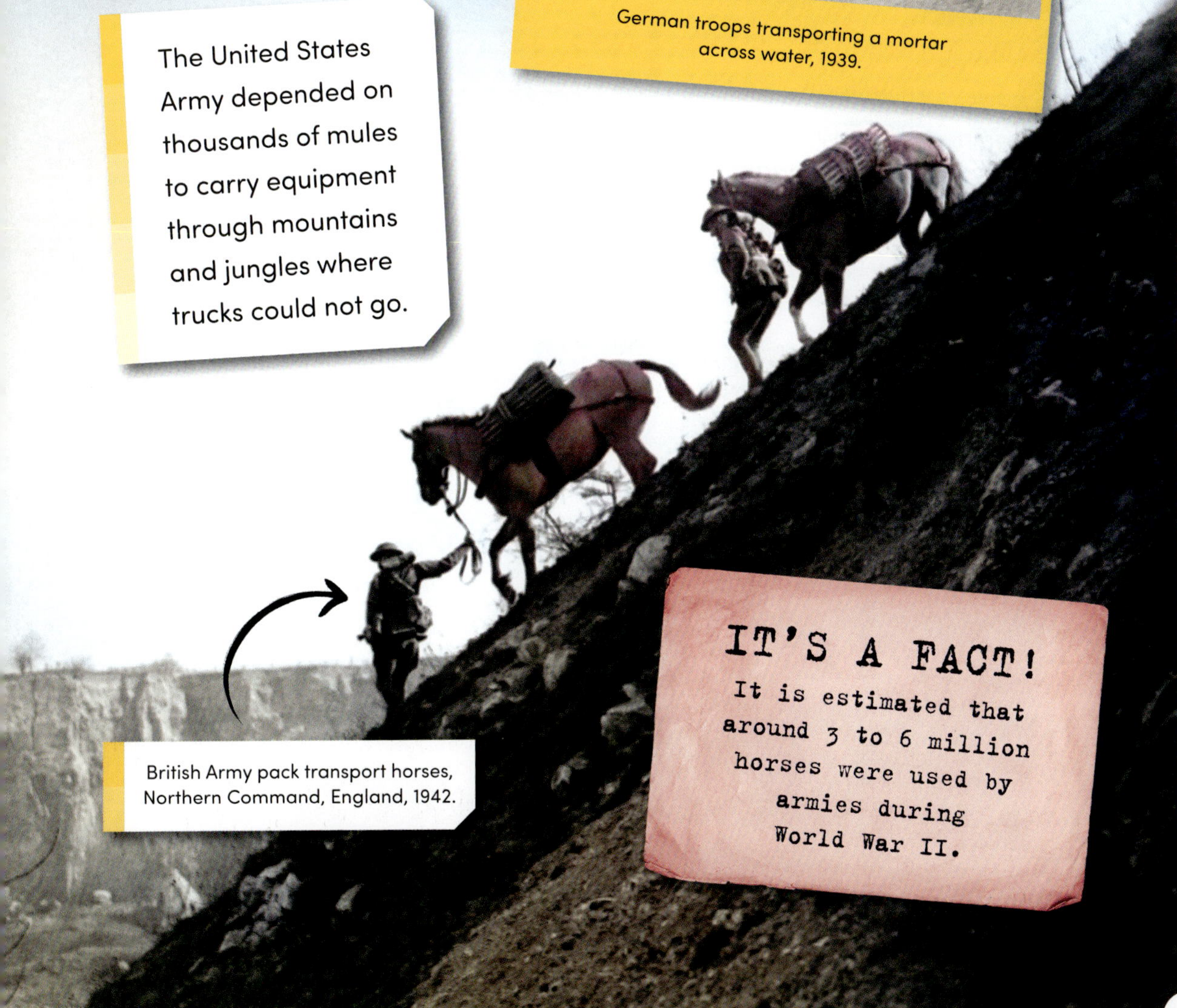

British Army pack transport horses, Northern Command, England, 1942.

IT'S A FACT!

It is estimated that around 3 to 6 million horses were used by armies during World War II.

CATS AT WAR

During World War II, soldiers, sailors, and civilians faced long days and frightening nights. Sometimes, comfort came from an unexpected place: a pair of paws, a flicking tail, and a small meow!

Although cats might not have worn uniforms like the people around them, they still played an important role during the war.

A US Marine with Sandy, a sea fort mascot, October 1944.

Convoy, the Royal Navy cat mascot on HMS Hermione, Gibraltar, 1941.

Aboard ships, cats helped control rats and mice that threatened food supplies and equipment. Pest-free ships were vital for long voyages across dangerous seas.

On land, cats lived with soldiers, factory workers, and families. When bombs fell and sirens wailed, these quiet companions often curled up beside people, bringing comfort in dark air raid shelters and crowded barracks. Cats offered calm in chaos, and in the middle of war that mattered.

Auxiliary Fire Service women with the station cat George, London, UK, 1940.

A cat's ears can still move toward sounds while it sleeps.

IT'S A FACT!

Most cats sleep 12 to 16 hours a day, so they spend more time resting than most other animals.

DID YOU KNOW?

Cats can jump up to six times their body length in a single leap.

PAWS ON DECK

Blackie was a sleek, black-furred ship's cat who prowled the decks of the British battleship HMS Prince of Wales.

This cat caught vermin that threatened the crew's food supplies and could damage equipment. Blackie proved an essential member of the crew.

Pincher, the ship's cat of HMS Exeter, held by a sailor, 15 February, 1940.

Alongside this work, he had another important job: boosting the crew's morale, especially on difficult days.

Many sailors believed ship's cats brought good luck and kept them safe at sea.

In August 1941, Blackie became famous when Winston Churchill visited the ship for a meeting with Franklin D. Roosevelt during the Atlantic Conference. As Churchill prepared to leave, Blackie padded across the deck and gently brushed against Churchill's leg, and he gave the cat a gentle stroke. A photographer nearby snapped the scene, and the image quickly spread around the world, turning the ship's cat into an unexpected wartime celebrity.

Winston Churchill greets Blackie, the ship's cat of HMS Prince of Wales, 1941.

After the visit, the crew reportedly renamed Blackie "Churchill" in honour of their distinguished guest.

Winston Churchill, Britain's wartime Prime Minister.

IT'S A FACT!

Winston Churchill was the Prime Minister of the United Kingdom during much of World War II. He was famous for leading Britain during the war, and his powerful, eloquent speeches.

THE CAT WHO BECAME A SAILOR

In 1949, near the end of the Chinese Civil War, the British warship HMS Amethyst was sailing along the Yangtze River when artillery shells exploded around it. The attack badly damaged the ship, and the captain was killed. Many sailors were injured, including the ship's small black-and-white cat called Simon.

Simon, the ship's cat of HMS Amethyst, with his Dickin Medal, 1949.

HMS Amethyst at anchor during Royal Navy operations in World War II.

Stranded for weeks, the battered ship became a battleground as rats invaded the dwindling food stores. Even nursing his wounds, Simon sprang into action, chasing the intruders and guarding the sailors' food supplies.

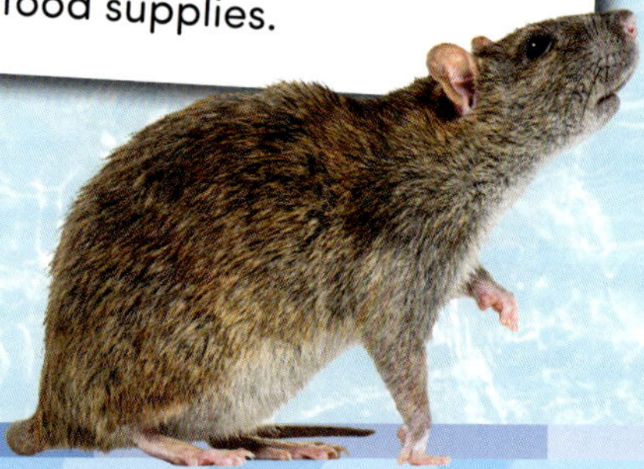

One especially bold rat kept sneaking away with food, until Simon finally caught him. The overjoyed crew proudly promoted their fearless friend to "Able Seaman Simon."

Simon was celebrated as a hero. His rat-hunting protected the ship's food and boosted the crew's spirits during those tense days.

The PDSA Dickin Medal awarded to animals for gallantry during wartime service.

IT'S A FACT!

In 1949, Simon received the PDSA Dickin Medal, the animal equivalent of a bravery medal.

Rats have oily fur which helps repel water and keeps them buoyant.

DID YOU KNOW?

Rats are natural swimmers. They can tread water for long periods, and even travel through sewer pipes.

MORE THAN MASCOTS

When we think of animals in World War II, we often picture dogs, pigeons, horses, and cats. But they were not the only animals that played a role in the war.

An elephant used for ploughing on a farm during wartime, France, 1941.

An elephant pulling supplies in Burma, 1943.

Across battlefields, jungles, mountains, and deserts, many other animals helped armies move supplies and survive in difficult conditions. Some, like elephants, pulled heavy equipment, or helped clear debris away, while other animals, like camels, carried equipment over long distances. Read more about elephants in wartime on page 52.

IT'S A FACT!

In Asia, elephants often helped move heavy logs and equipment through dense jungles.

In military camps, goats were sometimes kept because they could survive rough conditions and could provide fresh milk for soldiers. Other animals appeared in even more unusual ways. In Arctic regions, reindeer pulled sleds with supplies across deep snow.

Reindeer-drawn sled in the snow.

Slugs can sense much smaller amounts of some chemicals than humans.

Scientists even studied creatures such as slugs to learn how animals detect chemicals.

From powerful working animals to small creatures living in camps, many unexpected and sometimes unusual helpers supported soldiers during World War II.

DID YOU KNOW?

Camels carried supplies across deserts in North Africa and the Middle East, travelling long distances with very little water.

THE BEAR OF MONTE CASSINO

Wojtek was one of the most unusual animals of World War II. He was a Syrian brown bear adopted by Polish Army soldiers in the Middle East. The troops raised him in their unit, feeding him by bottle as a cub.

Wojtek the Soldier Bear at Edinburgh Zoo, 1950s.

As he grew bigger, Wojtek followed the soldiers everywhere. He rode in trucks, slept in tents, and even learned to salute.

Wojtek the Soldier Bear memorial, Edinburgh, 2022.

Because he traveled everywhere with the unit, Wojtek was officially enlisted as a soldier so he could move with the army.

In 1944, the Polish unit fought in the Battle of Monte Cassino in Italy. Soldiers carried heavy crates of artillery shells up steep slopes. Wojtek helped by lifting crates of shells and carrying them to the front lines like the men beside him.

The Benedictine Abbey of Monte Cassino in Italy.

Memorial statue of Wojtek the Soldier Bear, Duns, Scotland.

After the battle, a bear carrying a shell became the symbol of his unit.

IT'S A FACT!

Wojtek is short for Wojciech, a traditional Polish name. The name translates to "happy warrior."

JUNGLE GIANTS

During World War II, fierce fighting took place in the jungles of Burma and along the borders of India. Elephants became important to the Allied forces, helping soldiers move supplies and reopen vital routes.

Elephants move timber to help build bridges in Burma during World War II.

The terrain made fighting harder. Thick forests, steep hills, and muddy tracks meant trucks and tanks often could not get through.

An ancient temple in Burma, now called Myanmar.

For centuries, elephants had been used in Burma and India to move heavy loads through the jungles. During the war, armies relied on them to haul equipment, carry supplies, and drag logs used to build bridges and roads. Their strength and steady footing allowed them to travel where vehicles could not.

Elephants also helped clear wreckage after bombing raids and remove debris from damaged buildings.

These gentle giants became vital partners to soldiers supporting the war effort.

A Japanese Army elephant captured by Allied forces in Burma, October 1944.

IT'S A FACT!

Elephants spend most of their day eating. An adult elephant can eat up to about 330 lbs (150 kg) of plants in a single day.

A male Asian elephant splashing in the water.

DID YOU KNOW?

An elephant's trunk has around 40,000 muscles. That's far more than the entire human body.

HEROES OF THE DESERT WAR

During World War II, camels played a key role in desert campaigns where trucks and tanks often struggled to travel.

In the hot, sandy landscapes of North Africa and the Middle East, soldiers relied on camels to carry people, supplies, and messages across vast stretches of desert.

Ethiopian troops advance with camels carrying supplies in World War II.

Camels were especially useful during fighting in places like Libya and Egypt in the North African Campaign (1940–1943) and parts of the Middle East Campaign (1941–1943), where long distances and extreme heat made travel difficult.

Camels can travel for days without drinking water.

Camels share the airfield with a B-24 bomber at a World War II base in Sudan.

Camels are perfectly suited to desert life. Their wide feet help them walk across soft sand without sinking, and they can travel long distances with little water. Soldiers used them to transport food, equipment, and sometimes wounded troops.

These hardworking animals helped keep supply lines open and armies moving forward.

A Bactrian camel can carry loads of up to 450 lbs (200 kg).

Camels are built to survive harsh desert heat. Their hump stores fat for energy.

IT'S A FACT!

Did you know the Dromedary camel has one hump, while the Bactrian has two? Most camels used in deserts today are dromedaries.

UNUSUAL ANIMALS, IMPORTANT MISSIONS

World War II encouraged scientists and engineers to explore unusual ideas. Some wondered whether animals could help solve difficult wartime problems.

Researchers studied small animals such as mice and rats because they could squeeze through narrow spaces.

Rats can learn tricks and solve simple puzzles.

Most canaries are bright yellow, but they can also be orange, white, or brown.

Birds such as canaries were used to warn people if dangerous gases were present in enclosed areas.

Some experiments were even more unusual. In dark trenches, soldiers sometimes used glowworms to produce a faint natural light that allowed them to read maps or messages without revealing their position.

Glowworms are actually the larvae of small flies, not true worms.

Not every experiment was successful, but these ideas show how creative people became when trying to solve the challenges of war.

Glowworms inside Waipu Cave on the North Island of New Zealand.

A wood mouse can jump up to 3 ft (1 m).

IT'S A FACT!

Field mice disabled German tanks at Stalingrad by chewing through wiring, leaving many vehicles unusable.

TINY MINE HUNTERS

Rats have a great sense of smell. Because of this ability, scientists during World War II studied rats to see if they could detect dangerous materials, such as explosives.

A trained rat searches for buried landmines in a practice minefield.

Workers stand behind explosives cleared with the help of trained "hero rats," Angola, 2024.

Although rats were not widely used on battlefields during the war, the research showed they could be trained to locate hidden objects. These early studies later inspired modern projects where trained rats help detect landmines in former war zones.

A giant African pouched rat learns to find landmines during training in Mozambique.

Today, organisations such as APOPO train African rats to locate buried landmines. Because the rats are so light, they can walk across minefields without setting off explosives. The rats' remarkable sense of smell helps these small animals make dangerous places safer for people.

A handler prepares a trained "hero rat" to search for landmines, Angola, 2024.

A giant African pouched rat rewarded with a banana during landmine detection training.

IT'S A FACT!

APOPO is a Dutch acronym meaning "Anti-Personnel Landmines Detection Product Development."

DOLPHINS ON A MISSION

During and after World War II, scientists began studying how marine animals might help navies underwater.

Dolphins were interesting to scientists because of their powerful natural sonar, which helps them find objects in the water.

Dolphins swimming above a coral reef. Some can swim over 20 mph (32 km/h).

Each dolphin has its own special whistle, just like a name.

IT'S A FACT!

Dolphins can blow perfect rings of bubbles underwater and then play with them, pushing them with their noses or swimming through them.

Researchers later developed programs such as the U.S. Navy Marine Mammal Program, which began in San Diego in 1959. Dolphins were trained to locate objects underwater, mark sea mines, and help recover lost equipment.

Dolphins love to jump, surf waves, and play together.

Their ability to detect objects with sound waves makes dolphins extremely skilled underwater searchers, able to find dangers humans might never detect.

DID YOU KNOW?

Dolphins are powerful swimmers and can leap high out of the water while traveling or playing.

BRAVE ANIMALS IN THE MODERN WORLD

Animals still help people today in many different ways.

Around the world, trained animals work with soldiers, rescue teams, and emergency workers. Military working dogs can detect hidden explosives, track missing people, and patrol dangerous areas. Their powerful sense of smell allows them to find things that humans and machines might miss.

Rangers on patrol in a destroyed city during a military rescue operation training exercise.

A visit from a therapy dog brightens a patient's day.

Animals also help people recover from difficult experiences. Therapy animals often visit injured people, bringing comfort and companionship during recovery.

Some modern naval programmes even work with marine animals such as dolphins and sea lions, which can help locate objects underwater.

A sea lion swimming in the Sea of Cortez.

A soldier with his faithful companion.

Although technology has changed the way conflicts are managed, animals continue to use their natural abilities to help keep people safe.

Modern soldiers use drones for observation.

DOGS WHO SERVE TODAY

Today, specially trained dogs still work side by side with soldiers around the world. Many training methods used today were shaped by lessons learned during World War II, when armies first developed large-scale working dog training programs.

A U.S. soldier and service dog honor Independence Day.

Lucca, a retired U.S. Marine Corps dog, wearing the PDSA Dickin Medal.

One remarkable example is Lucca, a military detection dog who served with the United States Marine Corps from 2006–2012.

During her service, Lucca was deployed to both Iraq and Afghanistan. She completed more than 400 patrol missions, using her powerful sense of smell to locate hidden explosives before soldiers reached them.

Lucca after receiving the PDSA Dickin Medal at Wellington Barracks, London.

On her final patrol in Afghanistan in 2012, Lucca was injured by an improvised explosive device and later lost one of her legs. After recovering, she retired and was adopted by her handler.

Lucca's bravery is a powerful reminder that animals have long played an important role in protecting the soldiers who serve beside them.

Landing exercise SsangYong, Pohang, South Korea, March 2014.

HEROES BEYOND THE BATTLEFIELD

Heroism isn't only found on battlefields. Sometimes bravery appears when people need help most.

Two extraordinary guide dogs, Roselle and Salty, were working with their blind owners in the World Trade Centre when the buildings were attacked on 11 September 2001. The two Labrador Retrievers remained calm and focused as smoke filled the buildings and thousands of people rushed to escape.

Guide dogs Roselle (left) and Salty (right), both heroes of 9/11.

Lower Manhattan skyline prior to 11 September 2001.

Roselle guided her owner, Michael Hingson, down more than 70 flights of stairs. At the same time, Salty led Omar Rivera through crowded stairways and out moments before the tower collapsed. Their bravery reminds us that heroes sometimes walk on four legs.

Frida, a Labrador, became a national hero when a powerful earthquake struck Mexico in 2017. Wearing protective goggles and boots, she searched the rubble of collapsed buildings for people trapped inside and helped rescuers find survivors, once again showing how animals can save lives in times of disaster.

Frida, a rescue dog wearing protective gear, trained to search for people trapped in rubble.

A guide dog working with its owner.

IT'S A FACT!

Guide dogs wear a harness that lets their handler sense the dog's movements. When the harness is on, the dog knows it is on duty and stays focused on guiding.

RECOGNIZING ANIMAL BRAVERY

Animals that serve alongside humans in dangerous situations are sometimes honored with special medals for their bravery.

A military dog with a prosthetic leg wears a medal for its service and resilience.

Maria Dickin, the founder of the PDSA, with Pat, a wire-haired terrier rescued in November 1942.

The PDSA Dickin Medal, founded in 1943 by Maria Dickin of the People's Dispensary for Sick Animals (PDSA) during World War II, is one of the most famous awards.

It is often called the animal equivalent of the Victoria Cross, Britain's highest bravery award.

Earlier conflicts, especially World War I (1914–1918), also saw millions of animals playing vital roles. Because the Dickin Medal was created during World War II, animals that served in World War I never received it. Later, to recognise their contribution, the PDSA awarded an Honourary Dickin Medal to Warrior, a famous British war horse, symbolically honoring all animals who served.

The honorary PDSA Dickin Medal worn by a horse.

In the United States, the Animals in War & Peace Medal, established in 2019 in Washington, D.C., honors animals that have served bravely in conflicts and peacekeeping missions around the world.

Kuno, a British military working dog, with his PDSA Dickin Medal, Woolwich Barracks, London.

A medal presented in the Animals in War & Peace Medal of Bravery awards, November 2019.

ANIMALS IN THE WAR YEARS

Just as today, animals were an important part of everyday life in America and many other countries during the 1940s.

Families loved having dogs, cats, rabbits, or even chickens. Pets cheered people up during the tough times of World War II. When soldiers were far away, animals made life at home a little brighter and less lonely.

Interacting with playful pets like these can lower stress levels in human owners.

Elizabeth Taylor with Lassie in the MGM film Lassie Come Home, 1943.

Dogs were a hit! In 1943, the film Lassie Come Home was released in movie theatres, telling the story of Lassie, a Rough Collie who bravely journeys home to the boy she loves. Lassie became one of the most famous dogs in the world.

Animals popped up in wartime posters and news stories, too, reminding people to stay hopeful and care for their animals. For children in the 1940s, having a loyal pet at home was a big comfort in an uncertain world.

IT'S A FACT!

The dog who first played Lassie in Lassie Come Home (1943) was a Rough Collie called Pal.

A Rough Collie, the breed made famous by Lassie.

PICTURE CREDITS

The publishers would like to thank the following sources for their kind permission to reproduce the pictures in this book. (T-top, B-bottom, C-centre, L-left, R-right)

Alamy: Associated Press 53L, 66R, 67TR; Allan Cash Picture Library 50R; Chronicle 7TL, 17TR; dpa picture alliance 58L, 59TR, 59BR; Heritage Image Partnership Ltd 48L; Eric Nathan 59L; PA Images 17TL, 46R, 64BL, 65TR, 68R, 69TR, 69L; Pictorial Press Ltd 70BL; Piemags 4BR, 29TR, 46BL, 52R; Janine Powell Photography 58BL; Gary Roberts 58TR; Smith Archive 4TL, 7R, 10, 11TR, 16BR, 18, 27L, 37, 38, 38BR; Ann Stewart 51L; Trinity Mirror/Mirrorpix 15; Hans Winke 40R

Bridgeman Images: Look and Learn 4TR, 7BR, 21TR, 30R, 36BL

Getty Images: Lt. Bainbridge/ Imperial War Museums 30BL; Lt. S J Beadell/Imperial War Museums 42BL; Bettmann 29, 34TR; Daily Herald Archive/SSPL 44R; Ivan Dmitri/Michael Ochs Archives 55TL; The Frank S. Errigo Archive 8-9; Heritage Art/Heritage Images 71L; Capt. Horton/ Imperial War Museums 45TR; Hulton Archive 40BL; Hulton-Deutsch Collection/Corbis 13, 25L, 34; Imperial War Museums 71TR; Pierre Jahan/Roger Viollet 48R; Keystone Features/Hulton Archive 32R; 2nd Lt. D McLellan/Imperial War Museums 9BR; Mirrorpix 31R, 35BL, 54R; Fred Morley/Fox Photos/Hulton Archive 19TL, 68L; Bonnie Jo Mount/The Washington Post 69BR; PhotoQuest 25TR; Popperfoto 4BL, 9TL, 41, 42TR, 43TR; L A Puttnam/Imperial War Museums 8B; Martin Sachse/ullstein bild 35TR; Sjöberg Bildbyrå/ullstein bild 26BR; ullstein bild 41TR

Courtesy of the PDSA: 14BL

Courtesy of the Royal Pigeon Racing Association: 28BL

Shutterstock: 1000 Words 39TR; aarrows 49BL; Ahsanjayacorp 43, 71; akimov konstantin 52BL; Guillaume Angleraud 55BR; Facundo Arrizabalaga 47L; Edwin Butter 28BR; Simone Capozzi 12BL; Rich Carey 61TR; Crazy nook 7TR, 55L; CTatiana 33; czfphoto 54; Digital creator 01 32BL; DixNoonanWebb/Bournemouth News 23TL, 28R; Dmitr1ch 46; DyziO 51; E LLL 21BR, 47BR; Element allqulity Designe 2L, 56BL; Everett Collection 14R, 24TR, 49; Dmytro Falkowskyi 20TR; FlyingRabbit 26R; Geo graphics 61; Petra Goeschel 49L; GPPets 71BR; Green Elk 63L; Hfakruddin78 51BR; Teelapon Hromchit 57TR; Svetla Ilieva 54BL; Yeongsik Im 65; Independent birds 53; Eric Isselee 5B, 15BL, 25B, 42BR, 44BL, 46BR, 47TR; Dennis Jacobsen 33R; KajaHiis 20BL; ladityarini 43L; Frank Lambert 16R; Andy Lidstone 45BL; Andy.Liu 19R; Antoni M Lubek 50BL; Madeeva_11 23BL; Aleksandar Malivuk 64R; Manokhan78 6R, 60R; Maui Topical Images 7L, 63TR; SanderMeertinsPhotography 33BL; meunierd 66BL; Monkey Business Images 62BL; paulmoorephotos 31T; Andriy Nekrasov 60BL; New Africa 11B; Klaus Nicodem 36R; Northcliffe Collection/ANL 12BR; Noska Photo 13BL, 15TL; Pandas 23R; Paul1982Dutch 16; peizais 24BL; Photoongraphy 66; Pixel-Shot 11L; PixelPerfected 70R; Anna Pozzi/Zoophotos 19B; Presslab 62R; Prystai 58; Pukhov K 7BL, 39L; Raju Creative pro 22; Rawpixel.com 28TR; SasaStock 67BL; H Sauchuk 49TR; schankz 27TR; Alexey Seafarer 43B; ShaziaPhotoGhrapher 11R; Ronan Shenhav 21; Sherbak_photo 63; Anurake Singto-On 2R, 10BL; smrm1977 17BL; smutan 5TL, 31BR; Ruth Swan 27BL; tomocz 47BC; Fred van Schaagen 39BR; verky01 22TR; Thomas Wong 57; woodHunt 56R; Rudmer Zwerver 6BR, 57BL; Used throughout: CCVideo; lestoneana; juragan lansa manual.

Wikimedia Commons: Library and Archives Canada 22BR